THE PRINCESS AND THE DRAGON

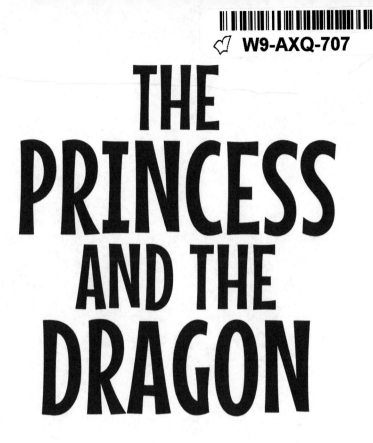

A . M . Luzzader

Illustrated by Anna M. Clark

Published by Knowledge Forest Press
P.O. Box 6331
Logan, UT 84341

Ebook ISBN-13: 9978-1-949078-47-3
Paperback ISBN-13: 978-1-949078-46-6

Cover design by Sleepy Fox Studio, www.sleepyfoxstudio.net

Editing by Chadd VanZanten

Interior illustrations by Anna M. Clark, annamclarkart.com

For Avee, reach for the stars!—A.M.L.

For my brilliant nephew, Carter. —A.M.C.

The real-life Princess Olivia and Princess Juniper

CONTENTS

Chapter One

❦

IN A FARAWAY PLACE, IN A FARAWAY TIME, THERE WAS A land where many wildflowers grew. The people there grew flowers in clay pots on their porches. They grew flowers in wooden boxes outside their windows. They planted whole gardens of yellow sunflowers, pink tulips, white lilies, and blue forget-me-nots.Even when nobody planted the wildflowers, the flowers grew wherever they wanted to. Everywhere you looked there were wild roses, violets, and dandelions. All through the spring and summer, the hillsides and meadows of the kingdom bloomed with color.

Now, what do you think this beautiful kingdom was called? The Kingdom of Hot Lava and Black Smoke? No. Did they call it the Kingdom of Very

Sharp Rocks and Dangerous Cliffs? No. Neither did they call it the Slimy Swamp Kingdom. All these names were perfectly good for kingdoms with hot lava and smoke and sharp rocks and slimy swamps, but the kingdom where all the wildflowers grew was called Wildflower Kingdom.

(You probably guessed that, didn't you?)

Wildflower Kingdom was taken care of by a very nice couple named Queen Jennifer and King Andrew.

The king was wise and always helpful. He was tall, had sharp blue eyes, and wore a beard of thick, black hair. The queen was gentle and always willing to listen, but she was also very brave. She had soft green eyes and long brown hair that she wore in braids. King Andrew and Queen Jennifer had two daughters, Princess Olivia and Princess Juniper.

The younger princess, Juniper, was six years old. She had big blue eyes and often wore her hair in pigtails. Juniper loved fancy drinks with tiny paper umbrellas sticking out of them.

The older princess, Olivia, was eight years old. Her eyes were green and she had a sweet smile. Olivia loved running and taking care of animals. She especially liked foxes.

Our story begins one night, just after the sun had set and the wildflowers had closed their petals. The stars were shining and crickets were singing.

Princess Olivia was fast asleep in her bedroom, which was decorated with purple and green stripes. She also had stars and rainbows on her walls. Olivia was dreaming about foxes and flowers, and it was a very good dream.

Just down a long hallway, Princess Juniper was asleep in her bedroom.

Queen Jennifer

King Andrew

Princess Olivia

Princess Jennifer

Juniper was dreaming about riding Sparkles the unicorn to the white waterfall in the southern part of Wildflower Kingdom. Her room was decorated in pink and yellow, with lots of hearts and polka dots.

Everyone else in the castle was also asleep. The wizard who did magic, the castle's chef, the shoemakers, the castle guard–all were asleep. Even the castle's one cat, Henry the Eighth, was asleep.

Then, suddenly–

Crack!

Princess Olivia's eyes flew open.

Boom!

Juniper's eyes flew open.

Boom! Crack! Kapow!

Olivia looked around her bedroom, wondering what had made the loud noises. However, seeing nothing, she ran out of her room to find Juniper.

Juniper also ran out of her room, clutching her stuffed llama, so that she could find Olivia.

Princess Olivia and Princess Juniper were the only two children in Wildflower Castle, and so they were best friends. Sometimes they quarreled, and sometimes they were cross with one another, but when there was trouble, they looked out for each other.

The two girls collided in the dark hallway.

"Juniper!" cried Olivia. "I heard something loud and very scary!"

Juniper hugged her sister. "And I heard something scary and very loud!"

"It was probably the same thing," decided Olivia.

The princesses looked around in the dark, but saw nothing. They held onto each other even tighter.

Clap!

Both girls screamed.

Karoom!

"Let's get Mom and Dad," said Olivia.

The princesses ran to the king and queen's chambers and woke them up.

Queen Jennifer sat up in bed. "What is it?" she asked. "What's wrong?"

King Andrew sat up, too. He rubbed his eyes. "What time is it?" he asked.

"We heard something awful," said Olivia.

"We're scared," said Juniper.

Boooom!

Chapter Two
NOTHING TO BE AFRAID OF

❦

"I'm sorry you were scared," said Queen Jennifer. "But everything is all right."

"It's just thunder," said King Andrew.

"Thunder?" asked Olivia. "Why is it so loud?"

"And why has no one told us about this before?" asked Juniper.

"You've both heard thunder before," said the queen. "But maybe not so close and not so loud."

"You probably slept through it on other nights," said the king. He got out of bed and put on a robe. "Come with me. I'll show you."

He led the princesses to one of the great windows in the royal chamber and drew back the heavy red velvet curtains. Then he opened the window. A cool breeze and the smell of rain floated into the room.

"See?" said the king. "It's a rain storm. Sometimes when it rains like this, there is lightning. And when there's lightning, there is always thunder. Thunder is loud, especially when it gets close. But we're safe here in the castle."

The princesses looked outside to see heavy rains falling in the castle gardens. Deep puddles formed around the shrubs, which were cut into shapes like unicorns, rabbits, and deer. As they looked out of the window, a flash of lightning sizzled through the sky, and a moment later there came the rumble of thunder.

Ba-Rooom!

Both of the princesses jumped with fright, but then they settled down.

"Ooh, it's *thunder,*" said Olivia. "I didn't know there was a storm. I thought it was a monster or a volcano or something."

"Me, too," said Juniper.

King Andrew closed the window and curtains.

"Sometimes I like listening to the rain and thunder," said Queen Jennifer. "It can be relaxing to listen to. The rain helps the flowers in the kingdom to grow."

"And after the rain comes the rainbow," said King Andrew. "If we're lucky, we might get to see one tomorrow after it stops raining."

Olivia and Juniper both liked rainbows. The unicorns that lived in Wildflower Kingdom especially loved rainbows. They always got very excited after a rainstorm. Both girls smiled thinking how great it would be to see a rainbow the next day.

"Do you feel better now?" asked King Andrew.

The girls nodded.

"I think I can sleep now," said Juniper.

"Me, too," said Olivia.

The two princesses went back to their rooms, and now that they knew the unusual noises were from the thunder and rain, they fell quickly back to sleep. Little did they know they'd be shaken from their sleep again the next night, this time by something much more frightening than thunder.

Chapter Three
THE RAINBOW

THE NEXT MORNING, OLIVIA FELT A LITTLE MORE TIRED than usual. Her eyes felt droopy when she came downstairs for breakfast. Juniper felt tired also, and when she sat at the breakfast table, she held her eyes open wide so they wouldn't shut again and go back to sleep.

Miss Beets, the castle chef, had made them a breakfast of scrambled eggs and crepes with strawberries.

"The scrambled eggs are delicious," said Princess Olivia. "Thank you so much."

"The crepes and strawberries are yummy," said Princess Juniper. "Thank you, Miss Beets."

Miss Beets smiled.

It was always nice when princesses were thankful. It made it much more enjoyable to make things for them.

Outside it was still raining. After breakfast, and after finishing their school lessons, the princesses asked the king if they could go outside and play.

"Of course," said King Andrew. "Don't forget your rain slickers and rain boots."

The princesses put on their rain things and went outside to play in the castle courtyard.

Everything smelled fresh and clean. The rain made the wildflowers bloom. Their colors were everywhere. Olivia and Juniper found some old copies of the royal newspaper. They folded the pages into boats and sailed them on the puddles made by the rain. Then they jumped in the puddles to see who could make the biggest splashes. The boats wobbled on the waves. The sisters were glad to have their rain slickers and boots on so that they didn't get soaked or spoil their clothes.

As the afternoon grew later, the rain slowed until there were only a few drops falling. Soon the sun peeked through the clouds.

"I think the rain is stopping now," said Juniper.

And sure enough, after a few more minutes, the rain stopped completely, and the sun shone.

The girls went back inside to put their rain things away, and when they returned to the courtyard, Juniper spotted something in the sky.

"Look, Olivia, a rainbow!"

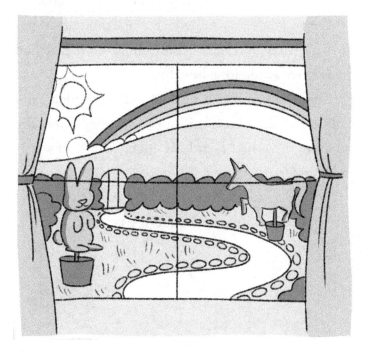

Arching over Stony Mountain and into the distant green fields was the brightest rainbow the princesses had ever seen.

"It's lovely," said Olivia. "I'm glad for the thunder and lightning because now we have a beautiful rainbow."

"Plus, mom says the rain helps the flowers to grow," said Juniper.

"And it makes the air smell so nice," said Olivia.

"And gives us puddles to jump in," said Juniper.

Both princesses smiled as they thought about how nice the rain had made things, even if it had made them afraid for a little bit.

They both went to bed happily that night, not feeling the least bit afraid now that they knew the rumbling they had heard the night before was only the thunder and rain.

But up on Stony Mountain, something scary and very *loud* was waiting in the darkness.

Chapter Four

✤

OLIVIA WAS PEACEFULLY SLEEPING IN HER BED AGAIN. This time she was dreaming of riding in a hot air balloon over Wildflower Kingdom. Off in the distance she saw the rainbow over Stony Mountain and the wildflowers in the fields. The balloon drifted over Wildflower Village, and the villagers waved and smiled at Olivia.

Then there was a terrible noise that made the hot air balloon sway and Olivia fell down in the balloon's basket.

Kar-Rooom!

However, after a moment, Olivia realized that she was awake in her bed. Something very loud had woken her up again.

Ker-Fooom!

Olivia ran to Juniper's room and found her sister still sleeping.

"Juniper," said Olivia, shaking her sister's shoulder, "wake up! I'm scared!"

Juniper blinked her eyes open. "Hmm?" she said.

Ka-Blaaam!

"Did you hear that?" asked Olivia. "What's making that noise?"

"Oh," said Juniper, sleepily, "it's just the thunder.

Remember? Rainstorms, lightning. Dad explained it. Go back to bed." Juniper rolled over and closed her eyes again.

"No, wake up," said Olivia. "That's not thunder."

She ran to the window and pulled back the curtains. Outside in the night, the stars and moon shone with a silvery light. But then came–

Kaw-Booooom!

"See? It's not raining!" said Olivia.

Juniper sat up. "It's not? Then why is there thunder?"

"That's what I'm trying to tell you," said Olivia. "It isn't thunder. It's something else!"

Juniper joined Olivia by the window. Olivia pushed the window open and the two of them looked out.

It was dark outside, but a full moon cast a blue light, allowing them to see the castle's courtyard and garden.

Ker-Baaaaaaang!

"There it is again," said Olivia. "It's definitely not thunder. It sounds completely different."

"It sounds like a monster!" cried Juniper. "And it's coming from Stony Mountain!"

The girls looked toward Stony Mountain, which looked far away in the dark.

Kra-Whaaam!

The mountains shook with the low deep rumble.

"Aaa!" screamed Juniper. "It's a monster for sure!"

"A monster?" said Olivia. "Aaagh!"

They both turned and ran to their parents' room.

Chapter Five
JUST A BAD DREAM?

❦

KING ANDREW SAT UP IN BED RUBBING HIS EYES. "HUH? What?" he said. Then he saw Queen Jennifer.

"It's the princesses," said the queen. "They've heard more frightening sounds in the night."

Princesses Olivia and Juniper climbed up onto their parents' bed.

"A sound you say?" King Andrew said. He didn't seem quite fully awake. "More lightning? More thunder?"

"No!" said Olivia. "It's not thunder this time! We looked out the window and it's not raining!"

"I don't hear anything," said King Andrew.

"Listen closely!" said Juniper.

The king, queen, and two princesses all held very

still and strained to hear the sound that had woken the princesses.

Juniper was trying to stay so quiet, that she held her breath.

Olivia was trying to stay so quiet, that she froze completely.

At first, the family heard nothing.

Queen Jennifer was just about to tell the princesses that it must have been a bad dream, but then–

Kraw-Booooom!

"There!" said Olivia. "That's the noise! And it just sounds awful."

"I heard it, too," said Juniper.

"Oh," said King Andrew sleepily. "That? Well, that's just Patrick." He lay his head on his pillow and closed his eyes.

"Patrick? Who is Patrick?" cried Olivia.

King Andrew sat back up and yawned. "Surely we've introduced you to Patrick," he said. "He lives in a cave in Stony Mountain.

The princesses shook their heads.

"Well, Patrick is a *dragon*," said King Andrew.

Olivia and Juniper's mouths dropped open and they looked at each other in horror.

Juniper dove under the covers.

Olivia thought about joining her, but instead she said, "Why is there a dragon in Wildflower Kingdom?"

"Everyone has a role to play in the kingdom," said King Andrew. "There are the farmers who grow food, builders who build buildings, and doctors who treat sick people or animals. In Wildflower Kingdom, Patrick the dragon does two things. First, he protects the kingdom from danger."

"W-w-what kind of danger?" asked Juniper.

"Well, we're not actually sure," said Queen Jennifer. "There's been no danger recently. But it's nice to know Patrick is there, just in case. Mostly, Patrick flies in the sky and looks for people or animals who might need help. If he ever runs into danger, he can breathe fire to protect himself and us."

"He—flies?" Olivia asked. "And—breathes fire?" This was the first she had heard about a dragon being in Wildflower Kingdom, and she wasn't sure she liked it.

Beneath the blankets, Juniper mumbled in fear.

"Yes," said Queen Jennifer. "That's what dragons do. Right, Andrew?"

But the king had already fallen back to sleep. So the queen just shrugged.

"But none of this explains the *noise*," said Princess Olivia.

"Yeah," said Juniper, poking her head out of the covers. "What's that awful *noise*?"

"Oh, that. Poor Patrick has allergies. Sometimes, when the wildflowers are blooming, his nose gets very stuffy. I'm afraid what you're hearing is the sound of Patrick sneezing and snoring and snuffling in the night," said Queen Jennifer. "It's loud, but from far away, it can be a peaceful sound, once you know what it is."

Kar-Roooonk, Patrick snorted and snuffled. The noise drifted over Wildflower Castle.

When Juniper heard the loud sounds this time, she pictured a nice dragon sleeping peacefully with a teddy bear tucked under his arm. "You're right, Mom," she said. "It does sound peaceful."

Olivia, however, did not feel peaceful at all. She pictured a massive monster who ripped through the skies and rained fire down on castles. In her mind, the dragon had terrible teeth and giant sharp claws. And Olivia was especially afraid of the dragon's eyes, which she imagined were red and fiery, like horrible flames. Olivia had never seen a dragon, but she was afraid of dragons. She was afraid of anything that could make such scary noises or breathe fire or fly overhead on giant wings. Olivia was afraid of Patrick.

But she didn't say anything about this. She didn't tell her mother, father, or sister that she was afraid. She felt embarrassed. Her mother was not afraid. Her father was not afraid. Even little Juniper was not afraid.

Queen Jennifer sent the two princesses back to bed, but still Olivia kept her fears to herself. Princess Juniper went to her bedroom and fell asleep quickly. King Andrew, of course, was already asleep, and the queen fell asleep soon after. But Princess Olivia stayed awake, her eyes wide open, thinking of the fire-breathing dragon who lived in a dark cave up on Stony Mountain. Every time she closed her eyes, she saw it–the huge monster with lots of scales, sharp fangs, and cruel claws. And those scary flaming eyes!

She did not fall asleep.

Chapter Six

A PROJECT AT THE CASTLE

✿

IN THE MORNING, JUNIPER WOKE UP IN A GOOD MOOD. She skipped down the hall to breakfast. She felt well-rested and energetic.

Olivia, on the other hand, was very tired. She'd stayed up almost the whole night worrying about the dragon named Patrick, who she had only just discovered lived in a cave in Stony Mountain. Even though Olivia had never met the dragon, or any dragon, she was afraid of him. She was afraid of him simply because he was a *dragon*. Olivia didn't tell anyone this, however. She had noticed that Juniper didn't seem afraid of dragons at all, and so Olivia felt a little embarrassed.

Juniper chattered and giggled while the two princesses ate their breakfast that Miss Beets had prepared for them–oatmeal and bananas. She was sure to tell Miss Beets thank you for the meal when she was done, and she helped clean up the dishes.

Olivia didn't feel much like chatting. She still felt tired. Still, when she finished eating, she also told Miss Beets how much she enjoyed the meal and sleepily helped to wash the dishes.

After breakfast, the princesses wandered into the great hall to play and read. When they arrived, however, they found something big was going on.

First, in the middle of the great hall, there was a big pile of beautiful flowers that had been picked from the valley. Off to one side, there was a large pile of baskets.

Off to the other side was a table covered with ribbons and bows.

Next, there stood a long table piled high with delicious-looking fruits, vegetables, and treats that had no doubt been made by Miss Beets.

The two sisters looked and looked. There were wildflower bouquets, piles of oranges, donuts, chocolate, and more.

Olivia and Juniper then saw their parents busily placing the treats and flowers into the baskets. Others who lived in the castle were also helping. The castle guards were helping, Miss Beets' kitchen helpers were helping, and even the castle cleaning crew pitched in. The great hall looked like a beehive with so many people helping to make what looked like fancy gift baskets.

In the middle of it all, Queen Jennifer held a clipboard and a quill pen. She made notes and gave directions to King Andrew and the other helpers.

"What's going on?" Olivia asked their mom.

"It's a new program!" said Queen Jennifer. "It's the first annual Wildflower Kingdom Thank You Day."

"How does it work?" asked Juniper. "What's happening?"

"It's a day I have set aside to say 'thank you' to all the great people in Wildflower Kingdom. It's very polite to tell people thank you every day. You two girls are very good at saying please and thank you. Now we have a day to give away some extra thank-yous to everyone who helps out all around our wonderful kingdom."

"So all these baskets are thank-you gifts?" asked Juniper.

"That's right," said Queen Jennifer. "There's one for Mr. Keller, whose cows give us milk. And there's one for Carlos the Beekeeper, who sells us honey."

"Here's one for Miss Cindy," said Olivia. "Who is she and what does she do?"

"Miss Cindy lives on the high road to the village," said the queen. "She gets a thank-you simply because she always has such a friendly smile when I pass by."

"You mean everyone in the whole kingdom gets a thank-you basket full of treats and flowers?" asked Olivia.

"That's right," said the queen. "Everyone in Wildflower Kingdom is so nice, there's a gift basket for each of them! Even you and your sister!"

"Wow, cool!" said Olivia. "This is the best day ever!"

"Um, a little help?" King Andrew mumbled.

The princesses turned to see that King Andrew had tried to tie a big bow, but instead he had become hopelessly tangled up in the ribbon. The princesses laughed and then ran to help him escape.

"We want to help!" Olivia said to her father.

"Yeah," said Juniper. "What can we do besides untangling you from all this fancy ribbon?"

"I'm sure we could use more helpers," said King Andrew, unwinding the last of the ribbon from around himself. "Go ask your mom what she needs help with. She's in charge of Wildflower Kingdom Thank You Day."

The princesses ran back to the queen and asked her what they could do to help.

"We'll do anything you want," said Olivia. "We can help arrange flowers. Or we can help organize the baskets. Or we can help Dad tie bows. Or whatever else you need!"

"Thank you," said Queen Jennifer. "That's very nice of you. We have so many helpers already. But I could really use help in delivering the gift baskets. There are so many baskets, and some of them must be delivered to the far corners of the kingdom. Do you think you two could help with the deliveries?"

"Oh, yes!" said Olivia excitedly. She thought it would be so much fun to bring people their thank you baskets. She was so excited, in fact, that she had forgotten all about her fear of dragons. She forgot her sleepiness, too.

"Definitely," said Juniper. She hadn't really wanted to tie bows, so she was glad to help out in a different way.

"Wonderful," said Queen Jennifer. "That will be a big help. Can you find the addresses on your own? You won't get lost?"

"Yeah!" said the sisters.

"Oh, and one last thing," said the queen. "You must stay together and you must not fight with one another."

"Okay!" said the sisters.

The queen nodded and then said, "Go and find

Mr. Lucas, and ask him to hitch up a unicorn cart to Sparkles."

Sparkles was one of the unicorns in the kingdom. He had a shiny black coat, and his mane and tail were a glittering purple.

"Sparkles will pull your cartful of gift-baskets," said the queen. "He knows the roads of the village best of all the unicorns, and he can help you find the addresses."

Juniper gave a shout of glee. It sounded fun, and she loved the idea of helping out with such an important job. Olivia was also happy to help with Queen Jennifer's new and fun celebration, but as the queen began to make a list of deliveries, Olivia did not realize she'd be going to the one address in Wildflower Kingdom where she never wanted to go.

Chapter Seven

MAKING DELIVERIES

❧

OLIVIA AND JUNIPER SPENT THE REST OF THAT MORNING making the deliveries. After each gift basket was created, Queen Jennifer added a big paper tag with fancy writing. The tag showed the person's name and address, along with a personal thank-you note from the queen.

The notes said things like this:

Dear Carlos—thank you for all the delicious honey!

Dear Miss Cindy—thank you for smiling and waving to me on the high road!

Dear Klaus and Sydney—thank you for coming over to dinner last Friday!

Once a new batch of gift baskets was ready, Olivia and Juniper loaded up a cart pulled by Sparkles the unicorn. Then the girls led Sparkles around the kingdom to deliver the baskets and notes. Sometimes, when the addresses were difficult to find, Sparkles led Olivia and Juniper.

First, they took a thank-you basket to Paul, who was the candlestick maker of Wildflower Kingdom. Paul had a beautiful pet fox called Sylvia. She had orange fur on her back and white fur on her nose and stomach. Her long tail was fluffy and came to a black point at the tip. Paul was a big, jolly man with a beard that was almost the same color as Sylvia's orange fur. He made candles and sold them to everyone in the village.

When Paul opened his door, he looked surprised to see the princesses. "What's this?" he said.

"It's a thank-you gift for you and Sylvia," said Olivia.

"To thank you for making our kingdom great," added Juniper.

Paul grinned happily. "Thank you!" he said, looking at the queen's note, the flowers, and the goodies in the basket. "Sylvia and I appreciate this so much! Would you like to play in the yard with Sylvia for a while?"

"Oh, yes," said Olivia. "But we must continue our deliveries. Maybe I'll come and play with Sylvia tomorrow."

"That will be fine," said Paul.

Juniper, Olivia, and Sparkles went on. The gift baskets were lovely and filled with fun things. In one basket, the queen had given some fancy lip balm and hand lotion. In another basket there were bracelets and hair bows. Some lucky person in the kingdom got a new pocket knife, and someone else got a red yo-yo. Olivia and Juniper would have been very happy to receive any of the gifts or trinkets, but they found that giving the baskets away was even more fun.

They'd given a basket to Mr. Lucas, who took care of the unicorns, and to Dr. Martha, who helped anyone who was sick. Every time the sisters gave away another basket, they saw the smiles of the people of the kingdom, and it gave them a happy feeling.

As soon as they emptied the unicorn cart, Sparkles would gallop back to Castle Wildflower to fetch more gift baskets. The sisters ran laughing behind. And for all that morning, Olivia never thought of her sleepless night or her fear of dragons.

She didn't feel tired or frightened. She was having too much fun.

"Okay," said Olivia, "the cart is loaded up again. Who is first on the list?"

Juniper looked at the tag on the next basket in the unicorn cart. "It says Patrick and the address just says Stony Mountain."

Olivia's face went pale. "Patrick?" she asked. "Like snoring Patrick? The flying, fire-breathing dragon who lives in a dark and scary cave in Stony Mountain?"

"Oh, I guess it must be," said Juniper. "Let's go ask mom."

They returned to the queen and asked their question.

She said, "Yes, it's for Patrick the dragon. He works very hard flying over the kingdom and checking for danger. He helps protect our castle and kingdom, so we definitely want to give him a basket."

"Yipee!" said Juniper. "We finally get to meet Patrick the dragon!"

But Olivia felt very afraid. "Um, maybe someone else should deliver this one," she said.

Olivia still hadn't told anyone that she was afraid of the dragon. She was still too embarrassed. So, she made up excuses to avoid having to meet Patrick.

"That's very far for us to take Sparkles," Olivia said. "Are we sure it's safe? Can Sparkles make it that far?"

"Oh, don't worry," said the queen. "The road to Patrick's cave is a little steep but very safe. Sparkles knows the way."

"What if it rains on the way there?" said Olivia. "We don't want these baskets to get wet, do we?"

"Not a chance," said the queen. "There's not a cloud in the sky!"

"Well," said Olivia, "I would sure love to go and meet Patrick, but maybe someone else wants to do it more than me?"

Queen Jennifer looked around. "It's nice of you to think of others," she said. "But everyone is so busy. It would really help me out if you two could do it."

"We're on it!" cried Juniper, she grabbed her sister's arm and headed back to Sparkles, who was patiently waiting to pull the cart full of gift baskets.

Juniper hummed a happy tune as Sparkles pulled the cart toward Stony Mountain. Olivia got more and more worried about going to Patrick's dragon cave.

"Hey, Juniper," said Olivia. "I've got an idea. Why don't we deliver all the other baskets in our cart first? Then we'll take Patrick's basket to him."

Juniper shrugged. "Okay. Sounds good."

It took an hour to make all the other deliveries, but soon the only basket left was Patrick's.

"Time to go up to Stony Mountain," said Juniper. "Let's go, Sparkles."

Sparkles nodded and turned onto the road that led up to the mountain. Olivia grew more afraid.

When they'd climbed about halfway up the mountain, Olivia stopped following the cart.

Juniper noticed her sister had stopped. "Whoa, Sparkles. Olivia stopped on the road way back there."

Sparkles turned to see. He gave Olivia a curious look.

"Olivia," shouted Juniper. "What are you doing? Come on! We've got a long way to go!"

But Olivia only shook her head.

Juniper walked back down the road to Olivia.

"What's the matter?" said Juniper. "Let's go!"

"No!" said Olivia. "I don't want to deliver this one. I'm afraid of dragons!"

"Ah," said Princess Juniper. "I see. I thought you were acting kind of weird. But that's okay. I'll just go the rest of the way by myself and deliver the basket to Patrick."

"No, we can't do that," said Olivia. "Mom said we have to stay together."

"Oh, right," said Juniper.

"Well, we've got to deliver Patrick's basket," said Juniper. "We can't go all the way back home now. It's getting late!"

"Mom did say he does a lot for the kingdom," Olivia said in a soft but nervous voice.

Juniper snapped her fingers. "I've got it! Just come with me, but when we get to the door of the cave, you can hide behind me so you don't have to see the dragon."

"Do dragon caves have doors?" asked Olivia.

"I'm not really sure," replied Juniper.

"Aren't you scared of the dragon?" Olivia asked.

"No, why should I be?" Juniper asked.

"Because they breathe fire?" Olivia suggested.

"I like fire sometimes," said Juniper. "You need fire to make smores."

"How about because they have sharp teeth and claws?"

"So does our cat, Henry the eighth," said Juniper.

"Then how about because they're huge and scary?" said Olivia.

"He probably is huge," said Juniper. "But almost everyone in this kingdom is bigger than *me*. And you don't know that he's mean and scary because you've never met him. Come on. Let's go. You can hide behind me."

The two princesses followed the path that led to the base of Stony Mountain. The closer they got, the more frightened Olivia became. To feel less afraid, Olivia tried twirling a length of her hair. That didn't work. She chewed on her lip. That didn't help, either.

When they had gone a little farther, they saw the entrance to Patrick's cave. There wasn't a door or gate. There was just a big craggy opening, and it was dark inside. Dark and scary. Olivia thought she could see dragon smoke pouring out.

Olivia grabbed her sister's arm and said, "Juniper, I'm scared!"

Chapter Eight
THE BIG SCARY DRAGON

❧❧❧

JUNIPER WASN'T AFRAID OF DRAGONS. SHE'D NEVER seen one before, of course, but for some reason, Juniper simply didn't think of dragons as something scary. Juniper pictured Patrick the dragon curled up and sleeping peacefully, maybe with a stuffed animal like the one Juniper herself slept with at night. Juniper thought that Patrick would be something like a big, giant cat–playful, fun, and cute. Juniper thought the first thing she'd do when she met Patrick was scratch him behind the ears.

But Olivia was the older sister, and she was now acting *very* frightened. Her face was pale. Her hands shook. Her eyes were wide. She was even crying a little. But now the moment had come.

It was time for them at last to meet a real, live dragon for the very first time ever. That is when Juniper herself began to feel a little bit nervous. As they kept walking up the road to Patrick's cave, Juniper felt a little bit scared. And by the time they reached the cave, she was as frightened as her sister!

"It's okay, Olivia," said Juniper, even though she was not sure that it was okay. "Just hide behind me like we planned."

The two princesses crept up to the cave opening. It was huge! Patrick must be a giant dragon to live in a cave so large. And the rocks around the cave were scorched and burned from Patrick's hot, fiery breath. A little smoke and hot air came from the cave. Olivia tried to crouch behind Juniper, but you'll remember that it was Juniper who was the smaller sister, so Olivia had to crouch down very tightly.

"There's no door," whispered Juniper. "How can we knock on a door if there's no door?"

"I d-d-don't know!" whimpered Olivia. She had covered her eyes with her arm. "I just want to go home!"

"I'll try just knocking on this rock here," said Juniper.

She raised her hand to knock on the rock, but she suddenly realized that her hands were shaking with fright.

"D-d-did you knock?" asked Olivia.

"On second thought," said Juniper. "Maybe we should just leave the basket at the entrance. He's probably not at home, anyway."

"Okay," said Olivia, her face still hidden. "S-s-sounds good to me!"

Juniper was just setting the basket down, when suddenly the giant head of the dragon appeared!

"Aghhhh!" yelled Juniper.

"Aghhhhh!" yelled Olivia. Her frightful yell was a tiny bit louder even though she hadn't even seen the dragon yet.

"Aghhhhhhhh!" yelled Patrick the dragon, and his yell was the loudest of them all. His voice shook the trees and echoed from the hillsides.

Olivia squealed with fear again and ran away, which wasn't very wise of her because her eyes were still covered. Juniper was scared out of her wits, but she was wise enough to take Olivia's hand, so that the two sisters could at least flee in safety. They shrieked and shouted and headed back down the road to the village.

However, Patrick the dragon was faster than the two princesses. He scrambled out of his cave like a giant frightened cat! Then he headed down the road toward the village, too. As he ran, he roared, "Oh no! Princesses! I've gotta get outta here! Scary little princesses!" His voice was like rumbling thunder, loud and very deep.

Sparkles only waited on the roadside, moving slightly to one side to let the princesses and Patrick the dragon run away. Sparkles rolled his eyes. Princesses and a dragon, both afraid of one another. He had never seen anything so silly.

As Patrick the dragon passed by the sisters, Juniper heard the dragon babbling about scary princesses, and so she stopped running.

"Wait!" she called out. "Patrick! Stop!"

Patrick stopped running and turned around shyly and fearfully.

He was definitely huge. Patrick was the size of three houses! He was covered in thick scales. On his hands and feet there were wickedly sharp claws, each larger than either Olivia or Juniper. Patrick's mouth was full of sharp teeth, and his wings were so large and black they could block the sun.

However, Patrick was also trembling all over. He closed his eyes tightly and covered them with his claws.

"Are *you* afraid of *princesses?*" asked Juniper in amazement. "Are *you* afraid of *us?*"

"Yes, yes," roared Patrick in his booming dragon voice, a few scared little flames escaping from his nostrils. "Princesses are so scary! Please don't hurt me!"

When Olivia heard what Patrick had to say, she uncovered her eyes and said, "We're not scary. In fact, we thought *you* were scary!"

Patrick slowly uncovered his eyes. Just as Olivia had imagined, Patrick's eyes blazed like two fiery coals. But they weren't exactly scary. Instead, they were bright and kind and very pretty. Patrick gazed nervously at the princesses.

They smiled back at him.

"Y-y-you're not scary?" asked Patrick.

"No," replied Juniper. "And look, we've brought you a gift basket from the castle."

"Oh," Patrick squealed with delight. "Well, that's quite nice!"

He began walking back to the cave entrance.

"Why were you scared of us?" Olivia asked.

"Because I never met a princess before," said Patrick. "I imagined that they'd tease me, or throw rocks at me, or do something mean."

"We'd never do that!" said Juniper.

"Yes, I see that now," said Patrick. "You both seem very nice. I'm sorry I thought you were mean."

"That's okay," said Olivia. "After all, we were afraid of you, too!"

Patrick laughed. "Of me?" he asked. He laughed some more. His giant laugh echoed off the mountains. He laughed so much that flames of fire shot out his mouth.

Then Olivia asked, "But don't you protect the kingdom by blowing fire at people and attacking them?"

"No, no," said Patrick, holding up one massive hand. "That's not necessary. I just roam around the kingdom and look for people who need help. If anyone's in trouble, I try to help out. It's a good job for me because I'm very strong, I can fly, and I can start fires or light torches and candles if it's too dark to see."

"Wow," said Olivia. "That's a great job. I'm sorry I assumed you were a scary monster."

"That's okay," said Patrick. "I'm just glad we can be friends now!"

Patrick looked in the gift basket. He read the queen's note, and then he found some tangerines.

"Ooo, my favorite!" he growled. Then he tossed the tangerines into his mouth–peels and all. "Delicious. Oh, and look. Your mother knitted me some winter mittens! These are perfect. We dragons get cold in the winter. Thank you for bringing the basket, even though you were scared."

Once again, the princesses felt happy to have delivered another basket.

"We're giving them to everyone in the kingdom to thank them for making this such a great place," said Juniper. "It was our mom's idea."

Patrick smiled. "That sounds delightful! Would you mind if I helped?"

"Not at all," said Olivia.

Chapter Nine

THE DRAGON'S SURPRISE

❧❦❧

DELIVERING THE BASKETS IN UNICORN CARTS HAD BEEN a good idea. Sparkles knew the village well and had no trouble finding the addresses. He had trotted from house to house quickly, and he helped the two princesses deliver lots and lots of gift baskets. However, Patrick had a different idea. He said they should place all the rest of the baskets on his back to make deliveries.

"I can *fly* you from place to place," he boomed. "It will be much quicker this way!"

"Oh, Patrick," cried the queen. "That's an excellent idea! This is the very first Wildflower Kingdom Thank You Day, and I didn't know it would take so long to get all the baskets delivered. This will save so much time!"

"I'm happy to help," replied Patrick with a bow. "Wildflower Kingdom is a great place to live!"

But Sparkles was annoyed. He snorted at Patrick. He thought he'd done a fine job of pulling the cart and helping with deliveries.

"Don't worry, Sparkles," said Juniper, patting the unicorn's neck. "You can come with us. We'll need you to help find the addresses!"

Sparkles whinnied and was happy again.

And so Juniper, Olivia, and Sparkles climbed up onto Patrick's large scaly back. The baskets were loaded up, too, and then away they flew. For the rest of the day they soared high over the kingdom. The views were incredible, and the deliveries were so quick that the princesses and Patrick got to spend time chatting with the people of the kingdom.

The last of the baskets were delivered before sundown. Patrick was invited to Wildflower Castle to watch the sunset and celebrate Wildflower Kingdom Thank You Day. And so they gathered in the court-yard and laughed and talked about the fun they'd had that day. As usual, the sunset was wonderful to see, and they chatted merrily with each other.

"Queen Jennifer," Patrick growled deeply. "The mittens you knitted for me are simply adorable. I can't wait until winter so that I can use them. I'm going to build the best snow dragon ever!"

"We'll come and help you!" said Olivia.

"Yeah!" cried Juniper.

"That will be perfect," roared Patrick.

"Hey," said Olivia, tapping her chin. "I just thought of something."

"What is it, dear?" asked the queen.

"The other night," Olivia said, "when Dad was telling us all about Patrick, he said one of Patrick's jobs was to fly around the kingdom and look for people in need of help."

"Yes," said the king. "That's exactly right. So, what is your question?"

"Well, Dad," continued Olivia, "you said Patrick has *two* jobs in the kingdom. What's the second job?"

"Ah! I'm glad you asked," cried the king with a big grin. Then he bowed to Patrick and said, "Patrick, why don't you show the princesses?"

Patrick smiled. His huge mouth was full of razor-sharp fangs, and yet his smile was quite charming. He took a deep breath and then turned to the far corner of the courtyard, where King Andrew had arranged a stack of firewood. Patrick leaned down over the firewood and let out a great, flaming breath, and in the next moment there was a blazing campfire.

Everyone clapped and cheered.

Just then, Miss Beets came out of the castle and swept into the courtyard. She carried a large basket filled with marshmallows, chocolate bars, graham crackers, and sharpened roasting sticks.

Everyone clapped and cheered again. They took up their sticks and began to roast the marshmallows.

Olivia laughed and asked, "Patrick, you mean your second job is–?"

"Yes!" roared Patrick. "My *second* job is making the best s'mores in all of Wildflower Kingdom!"

PLEASE LEAVE A REVIEW

Thank you for reading this book. We hope you enjoyed it! We would really appreciate it if you would please take a moment to review *The Princess and the Dragon* on Amazon, Goodreads, or other retail sites. Thank you!

WWW.AMLUZZADER.COM

- blog
- freebies
- newsletter
- contact info

About the Author

A.M. Luzzader is an award-winning children's author who writes chapter books and middle grade books.

She specializes in writing books for preteens. A.M.'s fantasy adventure series 'A Mermaid in Middle Grade' is a magical coming of age book series for ages 8-12. She is also the author of the 'Hannah Saves the World' series, which is a children's mystery adventure, also for ages 8-12. Her Magic Schools for Girls Chapter books are illustrated chapter books for ages 6-8.

A.M. decided she wanted to write fun stories for kids when she was still a kid herself. By the time she was in fourth grade, she was already writing short stories. In fifth grade, she bought a typewriter at a garage sale to put her words into print, and in sixth grade she added illustrations.

Now that she has decided what she wants to be when she grows up, A.M. writes books for girls and boys full time. She was selected as the Writer of the Year in 2019-2020 by the League of Utah Writers.

A.M. is the mother of a 10-year-old and a 13-year-old who often inspire her stories. She lives with her husband and children in northern Utah. She is a devout cat person and avid reader.

A.M. Luzzader's books are appropriate for ages 5-12. Her chapter books are intended for kindergarten to third grade, and her middle grade books are for third grade through sixth grade. Find out more about A.M., sign up to receive her newsletter, and get special offers at her website: www.amluzzader.com.

 facebook.com/a.m.luzzader

amazon.com/author/amluzzader

About the Illustrator

Anna M. Clark is an artist who loves to draw, tell stories, and buy journals. She has worked as a baker, a math tutor, a security guard, an art teacher, and works now as an illustrator and artist!

She has traveled through Southeast Asia, was born on Halloween (the best holiday ever), and loves to create large chalk art murals. Anna lives with her husband in their cute apartment in Logan, Utah, with their beautiful basil plant.

Explore more of Anna M. Clark's work and her current projects at her website: annamclarkart.com.

OTHER BOOKS BY
A.M. Luzzader

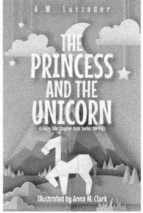

A Fairy Tale Chapter Book Series for Kids

For ages
6-8

OTHER BOOKS BY
A.M. Luzzader

A Magic School for Girls
Chapter Book

For ages
6-8

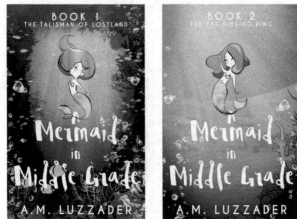

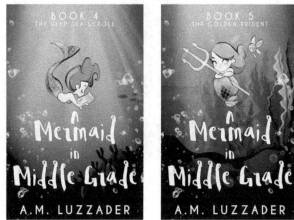
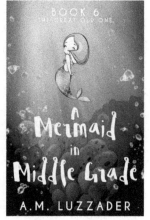

OTHER BOOKS BY
A.M. Luzzader

Hannah Saves the World
Books 1–3

For ages
8-12

OTHER BOOKS BY
A.M. Luzzader

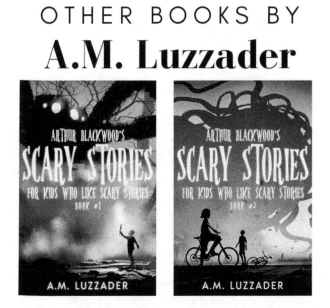

Arthur Blackwood's Scary Stories
for Kids Who Like Scary Stories

Releasing
2021-
2022

For ages
8-12